JOURNEY OF 8

New Beginnings

Charlotte Sun

Charlotte Sun

Book and Cover design by Aja
First Edition : January 2020

Charlotte Sun

Birth to Sun

We all birth dreams
We incubate dreams
It's not until we nourish the seed for
Growth
To ultimately giving birth to our Future

Acknowledgments

I want to give my love and appreciation to my beautiful daughters Tamerisk, Bria, and Maia for being such creative and loving daughters.

Thanking my loving and supportive sista friend Ida Clowney who walked me through this journey. Each day she gave me inspiration to keep writing.

I want to give a gracious Thank You Aja Graves who coached me through this journey to write my first inspirational poetry book.

My mom who has always been supportive of my creative outlets and has grown to be such a spiritual inspiration with Faith.

I want to thank the man that I fell in love with and gave me a different outlook of how to Love Myself and that Healing through my pain gave me a light of words. You have given me A Ray of Light I needed to start a Journey of New Beginnings.

I want to Thank The Most High, Creator of the

Universe who has bestowed me with a gift to inspire.

Dear Enemy

My Faith & The Prayers Within

Can Move Mountains.

The Creator Has Shaped Me Into A Warrior.

The Tribal Drums and The Spears Are Coming Your Way.

You Can't Shake Me or Move Me Because I Rise.

I See Lands of Unity and Chariots of Kings and Queens by Their Sides.

Children Protected by Lion King and The Head of The Serpent
Dragged by The Beautiful Mandrill.

You See Enemy of Many Names.

I Have Bloomed into A Beautiful Flower Violet.

Royalty You Can't Stop!

I Rise To Every Obstacle and Challenge I Face.

God walks with me and carries me when I Fall.

I Praise!

I Rise!

I Am Warrior!

Pain

Walking in the pain shatters me apart as the broken glass can't piece the recognition of sorrow.

Yet, calling on the almighty breaks generational curses.
My knees weaken to the bone marrow of sins.

Sins of the hollow shell and dim lights prance for just a moment.

I praise the Almighty to call on doors to open.

Delivering Daily Praise to the answered prayers and the deliverance of what was a dark place and damnation.

Struggles of the demons that whispered doubts and despair. Whispering with laughter to give up.

Whispering the enchantments of No Hope Spells.

Whispering for No Love to enter the heart and the crimson brick oven of bones' deception.

I stand mighty to praise the almighty creator to wipe the tears of sorrow.

The Whisper of the Angels to Get Up and stand firm for victory that the Creator promised.

The aches of trials start to whither and the storms began to break.

The clouds separate and The Rainbow appears.
I call on The Rights of Victory.

The Angels of Hope
Angels of Praise
Standing Still with No Waver Faith.

Broken Lies

You came into my life with Wings of an Angel
Only to become to Broken Lies

Bringing me joy of childhood Games of
Yesterday.
Yet, the games were broken and ended from
a toss of
Broken lies.

I gave you my heart, the soaring spirit and my
soul of gold
Only to receive Broken Lies.

My grace was stationed for you
Never knew of your blue and strongholds of
prancing spirits

Would drag you to a noise of unknown
chatter.
Chatter of Doubts, "Take your Time."
Time taken of mischievous bondage.

Your Charismatic Words of Genuine Diamonds
"I Love You, O.K.E.Y.T.A, I Always Loved You & I
Want to be with you Forever.
My Heart Cries and Lies Still.

Trust has been torn
Internal Peace disrupted by **Broken Lies**.
Chipped Excuses of Pain but Pain was Mutual
Healing of Togetherness.

Now my only hope is that my heart mends to
beat like the African Drum of Warrior.

Warrior Drums to Beat the Storm of Past and
Ends
Of Broken Lies

Seeking the **Beautiful Butterfly**.
She will **Fly** Away
Knowing **She** is **Worthy** & **Strong**

She is a Blossom and The Broken Lies will cry
Why?

Butterfly has Gone not **Tomorrow**

But Today!!

No More Broken Lies.

"Lava of Life"

Seconds Pass ... In the Instance
My mind becomes weary
Overload of trials control the bosom of
accomplishment
Minutes Travel. Lightning Bolt Strikes
The shock of the current makes brainwaves
prevail to reboot

Download begins words penetrate
Inducing an eruption of knowledge
Seizing a realization that life has been reborn
Hours have past

Crying to exhale updates
Stimulates the thirst for Knowledge
Stimulates the thirst for Freedom

Freedom to expand my random-Access
Memory
The Climax oozes to the infinite tutorial of
content, Information & Meaning

Sustaining

Sustaining

Constant, Constant,

Constant!

Volcanic Eruption

Causing

The Lava of Life.

Cosmic Love

Imagine yourself taking flight on a dynamic Rocket

Where the heavens open and the stars illuminate

For this flight is to encounter Spiritual Chemistry.

Although soaring through space you are not closer to the heavens.

To Achieve Spiritual Chemistry you have to inhale the Stars of Purpose.

The star, **Open** is to acquaint chance

The Star, **Soul** captures Love

The Star, **Trinity** allows compassion, honesty, grace, and wisdom

The Star, **Desire** embraces, Seduction, & Passion

Sparks Fly, Fireworks begin... Spiritual Chemistry

Creates Cosmic Love ...

Tasteless

Taste the mind of passion

Taste the smell of seduction

Taste the smell of sex that soars through the air

Stimulate the mind of the beautiful connection of a man and woman

The bond that can't be undone during the consummated act

Kissing, caressing, and desiring the fire deep within

The sound of ecstasy that races the heart

Love that erupts after pleasure

The taste of now

The taste of life

The taste of less

STAN BACK AGAINST TIME

Don't you dare say you love me!

Don't you dare declare that you miss me!

The Hour Glass shatters with sands of time.

My thought of you travels through space

Portraying Yourself a King.

A King of Lies, A King of Seduction, A King of Rule.

A King that STANDS BACK from Love And yet a
king, Is not a King, without A Queen.

So now you wonder WHY? There's thunder.
The Roar for more…No! No! No!
Why not explore with thyself and mate?

So you see a king is! A King! When, with-his-Queen.
His Queen! ----His Queen!
(STAN BACK) is what I'm forced to do
So, while I await … Faith... Faith … is my superglue

Holds me to you.

I Buried You

Memories of Sorrow, Pain, Deception and the toxic waste you passed through my atmospheric cavity.

The Grave of Cold-Hearted Blues and the Dark Sparrow that fell from the sky.

Can I ever forgive you for the death of my virtue, spirit, and soul you cast into the flames of hollow?

My Soul illuminated upon your discompose spirit as I buried you today.

The Remembrance that seemed to be glorified and yet only a depiction of my own insecurities.

The Tears of Bottomless Ends, the Wings of Chance, and the Spring of Water to the True Clarity of Redemption.

Lasting Shadows of Valley of Death Stops in its Tracks.

The Belly of the Whale as the Blubber of My Blubber

Lied into a Fossil of the sea.

My Fossil detailed of only just that inside representing the soul of denial, mistrust, and tyranny.

Tears of Hate only betrayed by the love I have for you.

Grieving for a dark cloud to strike lightning upon your grim.

You see it's only fair

I Buried You.

Not tomorrow but today.

Not last but first.

Understanding that every word was a hiss and every last cry was the kiss of my last breath.

I buried you and the resurrection of my soul is fed by the spirit of the sea.

I am Free to Be Me!

I am Free to Be Loved!

I am Free Like the Eagle that Soars the Open Sky.

Dear Universe,

I wanted to find Divine. So she can explain why cosmic appeared to me. The universe then said to find Divine there is a few stars to meet. I said," Well the stars have appeared in a vast ray of light and I can't seem to stop them. The Universe then said," Every star you will meet will point to **Purpose.**"

I was very perplexed and said," Yet, I need to know where Divine is to ask why cosmic appeared." Universe then said "When you meet every star and turn to **Purpose** you will see Divine. This will answer your question of why cosmic appeared."

I followed the Universe's instructions and met every star and yet, I still didn't see **Purpose.** I repeated the steps and each time I failed to see **Purpose.** Yet, this last time I asked the Universe," Why do you have me going through each step.?"

Yet, Divine has not come forward to answer

my question. The Universe said, "When You Have Not Opened Your Heart and Listened Divine will wait for **Purpose**. You see Each Star. Each Step is Divine and without Purpose she is Dim. Cosmic only appears when you are open to see everything that is good. Everything that is good shall follow and is **Divine**. Divine carries Cosmic to appear only for those who know me **The Universe.**"

As I Am

Reborn to The Sun and The Orion Sets for The
Moon
To Begin to Glow

My Heart Settles As It Intertwines Like Vines

Yet It Still Climbs to The Grace of My Mindset

To know That I Am Love

The Love That Craved For A Genuine Mate

That The Soul Searched

Long For The Time Is Of Now.

As I Am
Again Reborn Not Scorned and The Rips That
Gripped
Are Healed and Sealed

I United with My Heart and Soul.
My Spirit

As I Am is Wholeness and Awakened by My
Eternal Light
and The Warrior I Am to Unite.

Divine Blueprint of Femi9

*Your mind is the blueprint of Joy, Love and Universal Order (Ma'at)

*Your full voluptuous lips are the beautiful instruments that create the sweet healing tones of healing Love.

*Your eyes are the Black Hole that absorbs and rids all evil and expels a crystal essence.

*Your smooth legs are the 2 great pillars where all creation comes out from between to 'seed the
uni-verse.

...You are a Divine Femi9.

 Amun

Synergy of Openness

When I Look at You My Mind Body and Soul

Intertwines with Happiness.

My Energy Becomes Electric Like the Towers of Ecstasy.

My Mind Opens to Mother Earth that Gives Birth to All Life.

Your Spirit is The Essence of Synergy.

I Gaze at the Galactic Stars to Praise that We are One.

The Yolk that Speaks Life to Myself
And Gifts Me You.

O.K.E.Y.T.A.

You have made my soul complete and gave me a reason too open my heart up and share it,

O.K.E.Y.T.A. you have rekindled the Central Sun in My Solar Plexus.

I am not Afraid Anymore

I am Free

You make me feel that I can achieve any and all things.

We will soar...together...as one soul, one mind, and all things

I Love You O.K.E.Y.T.A.

My Body gets lost in Your Wonderful Smile

The Tone of Your Voice Brings Tone to My Climax never Reached.

I am Weak. I reach for something.

I cannot grab for its not there, because what

has been trying to reach for all this time is now a part of me.

Which is You Okeyta.

The Promise

As the sun rises in the East and Sets in the West, so do you control the movements of the primeval waters that all things come from.

So because of this you will always have my heart and Love.

The mere tone of your voice resonates inside my body, building my foundation even stronger with love for you.

Always remember that you are a precious gift and Jewel. Never forget that!

Amun

I end this that We Are In Love and True Love Finds Its Way... The Journey Continues **8**

Shadow Hour of Fire

As My Lips Press Against Yours.

My Body Begins to Quiver to Ecstasy.

Remembering Each Conversation that Bench Pressed My Ear.

Wondering More and More Each Day of Your Near Kiss

I Wish Deeply of Thoughts of Your Body Submerged With Mine.

Oh! How The Twisted Tongue of Your Glory.

Makes Me Wet with the Quench of Burst or Maybe Thirst of Your Love Muscle.

Mmm!!! How Hypnotic, the Erotic Sounds of The Black Snake Moan … You Gift My Body to Feel Naughty.

Yet, That's The Maca That Serenades to The Brigade of Our Love.

So Baby Do You Want to Water My Flower or Slither Me
Again in A Wrap Hold to Fold in Me.

You Won Me and Tongue Tied Me Every Way.

Love Me Always 100 Ways to The Shadow Hour of Fire.

Eternal Merge

My body gets lost in Your wonderful smile.

Your tone of your voice brings my soul to a climax never reached.

I am weak.

I reach for something; I cannot grab it for it is not there, because what have been trying

to reach for all this time is now a part of me ... which is you O.Key.Ta

Amun

O.KEY.TA Love

You have made my soul complete and gave me a reason to open my heart up and share it.
O.KEY.TA you have rekindled the Central Sun in my solar plexus.

*I am not Afraid Anymore

I am not nervous Anymore

I AM FREE.

You make me feel that I can achieve any and all things.

We will soar together...as one soul, one mind and one Love.

I LOVE YOU O.KEY.TA

Amun

My Sunrise

You're my Sunrise
Looking At All The Transitions in My Life.
I Can Honestly Say That There is A Peace In My
Heart that I Have You.

It's Refreshing to Know that You Make
Laughter Spill Out Of Me.
You Make Love Pour Without Holding Back
without Judgment.

You Make My Spirit Play Joyously Like Children
in the Playground.

Is This The In Love That We Both Yearned For?
Absolutely Even Better Than I Imagined.

I Thank the Most High on This Friday.
A Friday That You Made the Call to Say,
"Hello!"
Now Its 17th A Month From the Wednesday
You Professed Your Love.

So Good Morning, to The Faithful Gracious
Man I Love.
Have A Peaceful Day Amun.
My Beautiful Friend Mate and Husband
Chippppperr!

The Universal Drum of Unity

As I Gaze Into The Horizon

My Heart Beats like The African Drums of The Ancestors.

Dancing and Rejoicing of The Spiritual Mate They Have Blessed Me With.

My Yearn for Love has Manifested into Solitude and The Peace Within

Blossom into the Purity of The Blissful Joy of You.

My King, My Warrior, My Ocean that Makes the Waves Speak of Wholeness.

The Waves Whisper.

The Enlightenment.

The Enchantment of Our Unity.

As Each Day Becomes Significant to Us.

My Love for You is Open to a Cosmic Galactic Star Burst.

Natured Oceans

My Love For You Is So Deep Like The Ocean.
Never Ending

My Love for You is the Wind Blowing and The
Whispers of Serenity.

My Love for You is The Abundant Fruit that
Sweetens My Lips of Gratitude.

You're My Sun That Makes Me Glow like the
Lightning Bugs of Summer.

Summer of What is Now.

Past is Buried.

Love has surfaced and The Spirit and Soul
have Become One.

I Love You-Nakuk aashuq antak!!

Deepen Heart

If You Look into my Heart

You Will See Resilience and Love

If You Look into My Soul You Will See a Vast Amount
of Growth

If You Wonder You Will Miss the Diamond That
Glistens

If You Only Knew the Words That Paint Colors of
Each Universal Task

You Would Know I Am Much More Than The
Shallow Box in The Corner and Cluttered Thoughts

Each Tear is A Purification to Become the Flowering
Pots in the Garden

If You Only Knew it's Not The Broken Glass in The
Foot of Yesterday

Because Today is A Stream of Happiness to know
What The Open Door to New

I Am New not only for You but For Me.

I Am not Alone I Just Need Your Hand to Say I'm
Here

I Am not Pain!
I Am not Closed!
I Am Solid!

Just Like The Beginning and Now to The Future
Look At Me and Keep The Rays Upon Me To know
Unity
Your Loving Care is More Than a Word its The
Thunder and Lightning of New Beginnings

Energy Force Field

We Receive All Good Energy.

We Block All Bad Energy That Comes Our Way.

We Manifest All Things That Are Great.

We Ask for Openness and One Energy That
Sparks Goodness.

The Moon that is Full and The Stars That Are
Aligned for Amun and Okeyta are Pure.

We Block those and Send Their Negative
Energy back to the Being Who Sent It.

Rays of Sun

If You knock Think twice

If You Fall Stand Tall

If You Cry Wipe The Tears Because The Fears
Follow Sorrow

Stay Uplifted for You Are Gifted.

Gods Sends Greater Purpose.

You Are The Ray of Sun.

The Moon is Just a Fool because We are
Reflection of The Sun.

Stay with the Rays of the Universe.

God Shines Upon those Who is Eye.

You can only become Blind to The Debris of
What Not.

Protect Thoughts and know that I Am All That is
In Me of Positive Energy

Awaken

As You Awake, Gaze At Me Like The Stars Above.
Remembering, the First Smile of The Conversation
we Abruptly Had.

Our Laughter's and Overnight I Miss You's and
Kisses Over the Phone.

When You Lie Next to Me. The Synergy of You
makes me calm. The Love I have for you give me
another Breath of Tomorrow.

Each Day Is A Lavender Smell of You.

Each Day is A Affirmation of Joy.

Each Day is Knowing That I Love You Even More
Than

Yesterday or The Day Before. You're My Earth
Balance of a Simple Walk down the Street.

A Kiss on The Cheek of Hope and Embrace of Faith.

The Universal Track to Peace and Wellness.

Even a Sigh or A Silent Stare makes me Glare to An
Etheric Message to The Ancestors of Thank You.
Because That Life of All Things is Beyond Anything,
We Both Can Imagine.

All Things Are Infinitely Divine.

Even the Uniting as One.
The Daughter That We Speak Life to Have One Day.
I Am Truly Yours!

I Am Truly Love! I Truly Choose You as My One That is The Number 9 and We Know Divine.

LOVE

Love is Awesome

Love is Unpredictable

Love is Sensational

Love is a Burst of Clouds

Love is Butterflies

Love is Oceans Blue

Love is Chocolate Sweet

Love is Candy Apples & Whip Cream

Love is Ice-cream

Love is Apple Pie

Love is Cream Cheese

Love is Cherries

Love is Strawberries

Love is Succulent

Love is Waterfalls

Love is Stimulating

Love is Wine

Love is just a Word

Love is Action

Love is Loyalty

Love is a Breath of Fresh Air

Love is Best Friends

Love is a Sunny Day

Love is A Brownie Sundae

Love is Wealth

Love is Joy

Love is a Soul Mate & Love is Priceless

Bliss Me

It's Not the Way You Bliss Me

It's the Candy Licks That Make Me Tick

Each Lick Gave Me a Sensual Gravity to Make Me want to Jump on the Cosmic Ride of Seduction.

It was the Glare of your Erotic Stare.

Is It Me or The Beast of My Purr or the wet juicy quench of my thirst to Burst In Your Candy Coated Drops of My Rain.

Keep Rising Baby Because I'm Ready to Ride to The Galactic Sound of Me and You Exchanging Organic Stars of The Cosmos of Intertwine Grind to Ecstasy.

Knight Skies

The illuminated knight skies
I could see him walking down the corridor
My heart begins to throb for I know how the knight
is to begin
He grabs me and forces me up against the wall
My legs begin to give way from the gentle kisses on
my neck
Passionately he begins to reach slowly up my skirt
arousing me.
He gently slides his fingers inside me
Moaning softly telling him to stop but meaning
much more
My lips begin to moisten uncontrollably
Knight begins to slip to his knees making it
unbearable for me to keep control.
Slowly parting my sea
A rushing wave explodes
Makes my body blooms
With every force of euphoria
Knight grabs and kisses my lips so gently.
I can taste me on his lips
Each kiss Each Caress I want him inside of me
My heart pounds like a beating drum.
I then whisper in his ear smelling the cologne on his
neck

I want you now I want every inch of you inside of
me
As he begins to glide his Beloved Love muscle
inside my flower
It begins to bloom and water
The Electrifying burst of his Throb begins to make
me geyser.
My Universal Light begins to Glow
Knowing that he is My Knight that Ignites
The Hora of Passionate Love

Dear Heart,

I wanted to make sure you were beating at a proper rhythm and ask you why you murmured. Heart Replied, "I murmur because of the inconsistent behavior you brought upon me." I was perplexed of the answer and said, "Can you explain the inconsistent behavior." Heart replied, "Well Your Worry has overworked me. Your Unhappiness has slowed my pace. Your Exhaustion has begun to make me rest more than I should. Your weight has enlarged me and I just can go on and on.

How about the relationships that breaks me and I have to repair you to be whole again." I began to apologize to Heart and Began to Cry. I replied, "Who do I need to talk to, to make things right between you and I. Heart Replied, "I need you to Search for Spirit. So she can give you the formula of Happiness." I then searched High and Low but Couldn't Find Spirit.

I went back to heart and said, "I can't find

her." Heart said, "Go to Soul and See if He Can Find Her." I then proceeded to walk down this long path. The path had vibrant colors and stars that danced. I was at peace as if I already knew the answer. I then came at the end of the path and There was Soul. He was Very Tall and Distinguished and I Really Couldn't See His Face. I Asked Him, "Where is Spirit I Need to Make Things Right with Heart." He then said, "Spirit has been with You All Along. The Path You took to Meet Me is To Show You Peace and Solitude. The Stars and Vibrant Colors was Heart because you made it right. Just by taking time out for self, Spirit surfaced to make everything right for you to meet me Soul. Your Heart is **Beating** at Rhythm of Happiness."

"A Beautiful Woman"

A Dedicated Woman

A Woman of Loyalty

A Woman of Gratitude

A Woman that Loves the Creator of All Things

A Woman that Speaks Life

A Woman that is Graceful

A woman that is Courageous

A Woman that Loves Deeply

What More Can I Say

Everything Delicious

Dear Beautiful,

I wanted to tell you I Love You. I Love you more than you think. You may not realize how **Beautiful, Courageous, Phenomenal, Fantastic, Sophisticated**, and every positive word that describes you. You are a Blessing.

Although, you don't see it. Pick your head up High and Straighten Up. Don't let your Doubts Consume You.

Don't let the spirit of defeat make you fall. I will catch you and carry you.

You don't have to let people define you. Your design was already a confirmation of Beautiful. So tell me what are you worried about? Can you promise me that you will Rise Above obstacles and Adore yourself like the Beautiful Butterfly you Have Become? Show The Electric Colors of Magnificent and Share Gods Gifts of Purpose.

I Am Beautiful!
I Am Magnificent!
I Am God's Gift!

Abundance

Abundance is the opportunities

Nourishment of the accomplishments

The driven ideas that birth the ordained steps.

That the creator provides.

So that the existence becomes clearer to the purpose within.

Our eyes become open, the spirit awakens to gratitude.

Black Joy

Black Joy is the recipe of the candy apples of Love.

That serves unity of the soul food dinner that our

Ancestors prepared for the children of tomorrow.

The dessert baked symbolization of the dark delicious

Brownies and the Cotton Candy smell of **Freedom**.

Miz Happi's Recipe of Wellness

Miz Happi's Recipe of Wellness

She Is Rejuvenation and Mental Cardio

She is Love That Charges the Brain w Vitamin C
for You and Me.

Her Charisma and Laughter Gifts Us with Bliss
and the

Chicken Soup for Our Regroups of Whoas!

Every Encouraging Word is Her Wisdom from
the

Ancestors of The Grandmothers that
Transitioned.

Her Courageous duty of Beauty is the Dearest
Friend that Stampedes the Negative Energy.

Her Divine Sense is the Smell of Lavender Peace.

Miz Happi is Divine, Peace, Wisdom, and Laughter of Her Clowney

Desire that is Wellness Within.

FlatLiners

Flatliners Dreams made of disappointments

Flatliners Conniving Ailments of Certainty and Wanted Failure

Flatliners Deceit of unwoven masks and graves that masked the bones of unwoken mummies

Flatliners Torment of crossroad tall tales and the spells that staple Frankenstein's wounds of unworthiness

Flatliners Darkness that walks the shadows of ghost that haunt the Soul.

Flatliners rose that knows that the living is enchanted to dispel the evil that lurks within

Flatliners is the crimson candy brick that tricks the treat but breaks the glass of looking in

Flatliners are just the ones who continue to grab the brew and stir the stew of the evil witch that comes to You.

So beware of the Flatliners that Rise from The Grave and Steal Your Joy but Behold

The Lightning Strikes Long Enough to End The Flatliners Sin!!!

The Message of Emptiness- "Greetings, I'm Healing "Self" I Need Time to Be By Myself.

Amun
When I start to reflect on the beautiful moments we shared together and the endless talks on the phone and video chats. My hora begins to glow and I began to smile and laugh likes a little girl playing with her dolls. Yet after the reminiscence of joy the reality sets in that my hora became a dim light of sadness, I try to grasp of the sudden dimness and the state of darkness that crowded our space. I began to read every journal of the Journey we were to complete as Mr. & Mrs. and The Sweet Kisses of Greetings and Meetings of Holding Hands and Eating Veggie Patties. Yet Again My Light began to dim because reality sets in. I am not open to see the grim but to stay light to a bright day where we can begin again. You see **"Love is Patient" and "Love is Kind".**

My Love for You is Stronger than You will Ever Know and The Words are not Words but Actions of The Kindness to Plant the Seed of Our Expansion of Life and Create Music of Abundance Joy and Perseverance. I can only wonder of the thoughts that come to mind. **Are You thinking about me? Do You Love Me? Do You Still Love Me? Do You Miss Me? My Wonders of Just How can you share all**

the Love & Joy and Just say Nothing. No Response Just An Empty Space. An Empty space of a Black Hole. An Abyss that no one can find you.

My Heart is Heavy and My Bones Begin to ache and My Blood begins to Thin Like The Bark that Falls of Trees. The Vessel of My Spirit is Lingering to Find A Valid Explanation of Why? My Soul says "Love" My Spirit Says "Forgiveness" to Heal the open wound that you embraced me with. My Love still cultivates the Breath of Life and Yet My Mind is Troubled and Weary.
Because Healing "Self" is a Term but not an Explanation of Why. Self can be *Self*ish *Self*less *Self* doubt, *Self* doom, *Self* pity, **Self** Fear...but Do *Self* Think about Hurt and Wounds of Others of Their **Self**- ish undertones and judgments.

Assumptions are the mirror image of "Self". We are only the Fruit of What We Eat of Others that Surround us with Unawareness and Unhappiness and a Facade. Brokenness can lead to Loneliness. Loneliness Leads to Darkness of Headaches of "Self".

We Mirror the Image of What we detest and don't see The Unconditional Love That One Gives because of the wounds of Fear. The Daggers of Pain and The Flood of Others' Loneliness and Sorrow. My Faith is strong and as A Divine Femi9 Woman I will continue to Pray and Stay True to Being A Loving Faithful Warm Spirited Being That is Not of This Earth and That The Universe Always Takes Care of The Divine Femi9

Unconditional Love & Prayers

Dear Sun,

I was looking for your sister, **Sunshine** the other day and came across the Clouds. They told me they wanted to continue to be Gloomy. Yet, I told them that I had seen sunshine and she was **Divine.** They were not Happy that I searched across the sky to seek high to find her. I told her all the testimonies that I had overcame. I also, asked why, did the clouds call out **Thunder** to **Shake Me**.

Sunshine began to explain that Thunder was a warning that Darkness Lies beyond. I began to take another Glimpse of the Clouds. I then began to count how many times Strikes Thunder. It was **8** times I counted. **The 8 represented Faith & Infinity**.

This concluded that I was on the right path and to meet rain who represents Purification. I began to wonder why the rain was dancing. As I became closer, I asked Rain, "Why won't you stay still?" Rain replied, "So I can cleanse you of weariness and sorrow. You have been searching high and low but now you are cleansed of Weariness and Sorrow." I thanked Rain and graciously replied, "Wait what happened to Sunshine?" "She is within you and darkness has stopped following. Breathe and Dance to The Sunshine within."

Enough I Am

Can You Get Enough of I Am

I Am The Drops of Rain that Continues

I Am The Stars that Captivate The Growth of
Celebration

Can You Get Enough of I Am

Enough is The Smell of The Honeysuckle Trees
and The

Bees That Pollinate the Existence of

Every Flower that Dances with the Birds

Forever remembering the Bee's that buzz to
perfect Harmony.

Can You Get Enough of I Am

I Am Everything and Much More.

Regardless of the Tardiness of the Busy Train
That Blames

Roaring to the shame of What Could.
I Am Enough.

Old Pair of Glasses

You say I am looking through the old pair of
glasses
But the Glasses contain the hourglass of time.
Time that passes to learn the good and bad.

You say I am looking through the old pair of
glasses
As You see a star and glare but the glare is just
the chance to glance at the future of us.

You see the New Pair of Glasses, but couldn't
observe clearly because you were blinded by
The pain of the old glasses you wear.

If you could only see the Glow of Happiness
and The Gems of Tomorrow. The stare of
explanation is she adored and loved you and
the Glasses you wear.
You say I am looking through the old pair of
Glasses and need a new set of eyes.

Yet, you never realized that your love had repaired the eyes to new. You see I could see clearly of how you were the "**Neo, The One**." I just knew and the old pair of glasses was just the hour glass to know my "**Neo, The One**!"

The "**One**" to Hold Me.

The "**One**" to Kiss Me.

The "**One**" to Call Me "My Love"

The "**One**" to Make Me Laugh All Hours of the Night.

The "**One**" to Give Me Everything and Much More.

Depths of Consciousness

My Conscience arrives in a depth of the ocean.

As my conscience descends each aquatic tune gives me unknown breath to the state of openness.

My life begins to intertwine of all the current events of happiness.

Love begins to kaleidoscope toward the dolphins.

Their embracement surrounds me to ensure each step of Higher Consciousness.

Peace and Stillness created a Reborn coral reef of Silence.

My Body was encumbered by the emotions of brokenness.

The Belly of the Whale Sonar-ed the Universal state of Now.

Yet, I continued to transcend to the bottom of the ocean floor.

My Awareness of Purpose transpired to Ascending to the Creator.

Blessing Me with the Enlightenment of Grace.

The Transmittal Dialogue of Greatness.

The Chance of Purpose.

Conversations of Wholeness

As I look into the well and the water begins to
have a conversation
Water shapes to ask questions of wholeness.
I began to grieve at the question and dug
deeply into the grave.
Memories resurfaced of each current event
that became shattered.
Distance struck and tears dropped vicariously
into the well.
Water began to rise to meet me for a more
personal view.
I was taken back and started to pour out the
shapes that made my life.
Each shape made the water shift into the
medley of my life situations.
With Constant tears I began to shift as well and
water gave me a purification state of
Wholeness.
The Conversation was a shape shifting

occurrence to realize wholeness is in life and
what you can make from it.
Water began to descend back into the well
with moments of Harmony.
It vanished right at that hour glass of time
Solitude Poured Upon My Heart
Appreciating the conversations of wholeness.

Blame Chain

I Could Blame Myself but that would be a Lie!
I Could Blame Myself but Self Pity would
become a Night Train
I could Blame Myself but Is it Me?
No! It's Chatter of Noise.
Pollution of People and Their Negative Dead
Pulse.
Their Inside Hatred of Joy and Chatter of Noise
Pollution.
Just like the Lead Poison of Flint it's a stint in the
Heart.
Do I Blame You?
No! I Blame only the Energies that succumb
the weakness of the state of mind.
Do I blame You?
No! I blame the pain that wasn't shed to light.
It lied dormant to the crimson flames of your
past.

Do I blame you?

No. I blame every chatter that scattered with
a smirk to hurt.

I Blame the grey man that looks in the windows
pain of insane trail blaze of intent.

Intent to Break Up the Happiness of The Two.

Who knew that it was True

But You Blew

Blew Away just like Leaves of Fall. I Ask Are You
Through or Do You Want Beginnings to Winning
of A New Tree of Life.

Life of Creative Thoughts Adventures and
Peace

Isn't That What We Gained?

Creative Bonds through Childhood

Yet, Stress of Adulthood Blocked You from
Leaping to Joy

Do I Blame You? I Blame The Game of Life.

Depend On Me

Sitting here in deep thought. Depend On Me is what you portrayed. Lies All Lies and Pride Sits on the street of Fear. I was acquainted with the man of your word
Yet, those words are buried and now I'm forever in debt to the words that we called Love.

The Shameless face only sets to the sun and now the moon is full and empty like the bottomless ocean. You see the sunset is the purest thoughts of how it could be and the rise of our bodies start chemistry of the mere tone of embracement. Moon howled to the wolf that prowls and embodies discomfort. I can only imagine what comes to the surface. Regrets of what could but should, stays paralyzed to the lies of fear. The crescent of the moon crumbles to each word that flowed through a natural spring of water.

The Springs become frozen just like the words you spilled in the cup to be full. I grab the cup to intake all the beautiful words of the natural spring that you bestowed upon me. Disappointment that the quench can't be fulfilled because it's Frozen. Frozen just like you and now I'm buried and blue. It's the thoughts that I can't bear to dare treat you as the uneaten stew that the wolf begins to devour. I am at the deep end of the word depend on me because you're not free to the bondage of everyone's word and the blurred page that rage inside of me because now the wolf has awakened and knows her pack. Depend on me.

Dear Fire,

I wanted to ask you where water lies. I have
been looking for her and search high and low
because I need to put you out. I am burning
with anger and regrets and I need water to
put all the anguish and pain that has taken a
toll on my life. Fire then replied "Go beyond
the mountains and over the hillside you will see
a canyon that has water. Before you get to
the bottom you will see a fountain that has
purification on it. Drink and then all your
anxieties and grief will appear. You then have
to wash every anger and regret in the lake
below. Grief will cry and anxiety will lie.

These are the state of anger and regret
fighting to stay. As you walk a flame will
appear and begin to dance. Stay focus and
don't be enchanted to dance with your
anxieties and grief. Continue to walk and
when you get to the bottom she will answer. I
followed instructions and each step was just as
Fire said. I began to weep because the pain
began to hold me against my will to walk.

The anxiety and grief began to lie and the
flame appeared. I began to kneel and pray

that the pain would just leave because it was too unbearable to face. My hands began to tremble the coldness settled in my bones. I began to take a deep breath and began to focus the lake below.

I walked with a sense of peace as I began to get closer; the water appeared as it was rising. I got to the Bottom the Water Rose about 25 feet it was blue like the ocean and I could see a light shining within. Water began to speak, "Why have you come all this way?" I replied, "To remove the anguish and pain that has taken a toll on my life.

Fire has been attached to me for a very long time and I am ready for a change. Can you put out the fire so I can release anger and regret?" Water then replied, "Step closer." I took a step closer, it engulfed me and as I was in the lake, I began to get cleansed. I could feel anxiety and grief leave first. It was a scream that I could hear because they were trying to stay.

It was swept away deep into the abyss. Then anger and regret began to wrap around me with their flames but water began to spin as if it was a tornado within. They released me and the burn began to cool like the breeze in a park. I started to sink at the bottom and I saw the light and it appeared bright like the Sun. My Body illuminated and my mind begins to open and I was awakening to Peace. Water washed me upon the shore and my eyes open to a new beginning.

Fire Lies

Heat of the Heart Beat

Where the molten Lava runs

Through the veins of ecstasy

The fire in my eyes

Dances to your wounds of loyalty

Passion burns my legs

Quivers to Pain

The fire in my eyes rise

As your fire lies

Numbness Awaits

Thoughts tremble of the unknown. The soil begins to boil of the unknown. My heart starts to beat vigorously each day knowing you're about to enter the space of time travel. Traveling back to a place where it all began. My troubling thoughts began to reminisce of how our universal travel propelled. Our Journey began of just a phone call to rekindle friendship and kinships that last through childhood.

A childhood that held memories of laughter and moments of trial. A phone call just a touch tone of the unknown. An answer that would change the lives of both a childhood dream and adulthood of reality that settles of a loving embrace. A burst of energy that would energize two long lost spirits and their souls that were trapped in a pit of pain.

That day was the life changing experience of the woman and man who had a universal journey that would stop in time.

As the spirits united, the souls became distorted from the time travel of past. Distance became the two and the woman only knew that as the sky was blue it became green like The Hulk and all that surrounded, began to fester into a black hole of deception.

Friends became foes igniting a nuclear eruption of deceit and turmoil. Boils of Job began to appear, and the ears began to hear what the woman, "I" could not bear A statement that would make her "I" fearful. As they wore Black Robes and chanted to the Pharaoh "Take your time", He began to Fear and share the baggage of the woman, "I" to the Slytherin of Harry Potters realm. As they chanted, "Take your time." He began to become blind. The noise became a headache and heartache of the rational decision of uniting with his Beloved, "I".

An Explosion of all the Love of these two spirits became a suspension in space. It floats slowly as they became separated in the time of the unknown. Now its time for the two to reunite as the Pharaoh begins the travel to the eminent place of Unity. As I go forward to the Future of Now the numbness awaits of what is truly.

Summer

Summers go but memories surface

Like the spring of April

Although Fall Leaves

Winter Glistens

Friends and Family Rejoice Because of L.O.V.E

Lasts Eternal

Each day Each Moment

Ease the Mind and The Spirit Awakens.

Sun

Brightness upon my skin

Melanated pop culture of the Soul Glow

Craving more motion

The Rays of Bliss

A Season kiss of sun

A kiss of rays shine

The beam of total infinite peace

Earth to Moon

Earth to the Moon of My Travels

More to Love

More to Give

Ready to Receive

A Gift to Share only to bear witness to Stars

Leaving All Radioactive Residue Behind

My Heart is Open to See illuminating Essence of Gravity

Face Off

I want to take the face off the man who masked the poisonous gas that was inside the body.

The body that gymed the depression mind state of the holistic mirage.

A vegan machine that starved the minds wellness.

A mirage that devoured every image to create madness.

A body that was transformed to perfection.

Yet, the mind was the blue balls that could not release the seed to true wellness.

Wellness of mind body and spirit.

The mirrored distortion of success.

The mirrored stagnant force of infused decayed meat within.

Starvation of the nutrition of love.

The depravation of words that cultivate rejuvenation of the spirit and soul.

The purity of water and the life that multiplies.

The quench of everlasting life through water and words.

But the face that won't take off the poisonous mask just to breathe and drink a glass of life.

The Birth

The growth of every positive thought goes through a trial. Each moment can be rejoiced. Destiny provides the character to overcome the polluted soil that incubates casualties.

New Beginnings

I bereave to the cry of pain
As I sit, I begin to breathe I begin to sigh
Tears fall like the canyon of Arizona mistaken
by Niagara
but the sins of your fear
Leaves me grieving. Thoughts of my aches
bring the catacombs of the mistakes of trust
How could you? Leo the Lion a coward and
the dreams shattered to a battered and torn.
token of a love that lies still. The thorn in the
paw that could not walk and just limped into
shame.
The Roar of nothing and yet calls of
entrapment of jealousy, envy, and emptiness.
Stuck in the cage of pasts that breaks every
tribal dance of unity and the Chinese New
Year of The Dragon.
New Beginnings as the twinkle star draws near.
Not only to bear witness to those that tried to
spell cast bearer of bad news.
They will see the Good News that the Universe
shall bring Unity and the Love that wasn't
broken. Just another token God rewards those
that have grace and the faith of New
Beginnings.

Thank You

I want to give a Thank You, to the relationships I have encountered in my life
Those have given me a new outlook of who I Am
I Am Strong, I Am Enough to those who Love me unconditionally.
The unconditional flaws, unconditional conditions that beings go through.
The life changes and uncircumcised circumstances that the universe unfolds.
I want to Thank You for opening up my eyes to the rise of the lies you have bestowed me.
I want to Thank You for enlightening me of just the woman I am.
You see a touch of your brokenness gave me the discernment to know I am God's Gift and that I have a crown and jewels of a Goddess. All the Creator has ordered for a Femi9 women.
I want to Thank You for the unremorseful pain that you feed me at the unbalanced dinner table. That last supper was the awakening of A Natural woman that can do all things through the Creator. The Creator and the angels that surround me. The whispers that all is good all that has purpose. I Thank You for removing the rotten carcass that hasn't been disemboweled and cleansed. I Thank You for the disappeared

fear of commitment I Thank You for the exiled treatment of silence. The Silence that renewed

my growth of my Spiritual outlook of who I Am
The renewed Voice of Purpose
The Renewed Joy of The Eagle.
The Courageous Wolf of the Hunt to Destiny of
Fulfillment. Fulfillments that are in tune with the
Creator and the universal connections of A
Divine Thank You.

FAITH

Faith is my stronghold to a journey of refuge

Faith is my friend walking along the tides of trial

Faith is wisdom assuring me that the path will become translucent

Faith is the effervescence of my inner self

Faith is transformation of the hearts of man

Faith is my sunbeam that soars the cosmic heavens

Faith is my rain that purifies the pain

Faith is the outcome of the persistent prayer you long for

FAITH is The Glory You Give to The Lord

Faith is Love!

Faith is Joy!

Faith is Peace!

Faith is Power!

Faith is Patience!

Faith is Pure!

Faith is Passion!

Faith is Triumphant!

Faith is Glorious!

Faith is Victorious!

Faith is you!

Faith is me!

Faith is in Jesus name we pray!

Faith is now!!!

Amen

Journey of 8

Raising above the trial my confirmation of the Journey stands with 8 of Faith.

New beginnings of my sun.

Celebration of the reborn purification of rain that befalls upon my sins.

Recognizing victory.

Peace, Unity of the spirit.

Reminding of the fulfilment of purpose.

8 destinies within the spirit resurrect beauty, courage, and perseverance.

Trials broken and buried only to the destruction of its rightful owner the Enemy.

Now at last the Rebirth of the Renewed Mind, Body and Spirit awakens.

The oceans of 8 hails to the Journey bringing the Rogue waves to withstand **Journey of 8**.

"Love is the Flow of Ocean's Blue"

"Patience is the
Bench of Hope"

"Amour is The King Who Reigns Victory"

"Still Standing on
the Mountains
Forgotten
Tomorrow"

"Grace tickles the
Heart to have
Faith"

"Forgiveness is the Pricked Finger that Throbs"

Charlotte Sun

"Fruitage of the Spirit the Orbital Breath of Life"

Charlotte Sun

"Manifest"

"Destiny
Universal Order
of I Am"

"Favor is all that
God Gifts"

Charlotte Sun

"Spiritual Divine
Connections"

Charlotte Sun

"Praise"

Charlotte Sun

"Journey of 8 The New Beginning of the Spirit Within"

About the Author

Photographer, Leah Johnson

Charlotte Sun was born October 8th, 1974. Writing has always been her creative outlet as she overcame struggles and challenges in life. As a single mother of three daughters, her perseverance and strength has given her an awakening of devoting her life to the The Most High. She has also been motivating others through her journey.

Journey of 8 New Beginnings is about how life goes through seasons such as despair, disappointments, love, faith, and all the emotions that happen through your life phases. The key is the outcome and the lesson behind the journey and believing that new beginnings arrive.